FOOD CHAINS

SEASHORE FOOD CHAINS

John Crossingham and Bobbie Kalman

A Crabtree Crown Book

Crabtree Publishing
crabtreebooks.com

SEASHORE FOOD CHAINS

Created by Bobbie Kalman

Editor-in-chief
Bobbie Kalman

Writing team
John Crossingham
Bobbie Kalman

Substantive Editor
Niki Walker

Project editor
Kelley MacAulay

Editors
Molly Aloian
Kathryn Smithyman

Production manager
Candice Campbell

Design
Margaret Salter

Cover
Rhea Magaro-Wallace

Consultant
Patricia Loesche, Ph.D., Animal Behavior Program, Department of Psychology, University of Washington

Images
Minden Pictures: Fred Bavendam: page 18
All other images: Shutterstock.com

Crabtree Publishing

crabtreebooks.com 800-387-7650
 In Canada: We acknowledge the financial support of the Government of Canada through the Canada Book Fund for our publishing activities.

Printed in the U.S.A./CP032026

Published in Canada
Crabtree Publishing
616 Welland Ave.
St. Catharines, Ontario
L2M 5V6

Published in the United States
Crabtree Publishing
347 Fifth Ave.
Suite 1402-145
New York, NY 10016

Library and Archives Canada Cataloguing in Publication
Available at the Library and Archives Canada

Library of Congress Cataloging-in-Publication Data
Available at the Library of Congress

Hardcover: 978-1-0398-7300-1
Paperback: 978-1-0398-7358-2
Ebook (pdf): 978-1-0398-7409-1
Epub: 978-1-0398-7458-9

CONTENTS

WHAT ARE SEASHORES?

Seashores are areas where large bodies of water, such as oceans or seas, meet land. The water along seashores is salt water.

Many kinds

There are many kinds of seashores. Sandy beaches and rocky shores are just two kinds. Some seashores are located in places where the weather is either hot or cold year round. Other seashores are in places where the weather changes with the seasons.

Temperate seashores

Temperate seashores are in places that have hot summers and cold winters. This book is about temperate rocky seashores.

A lot of life

Rocky seashores are home to a wide variety of plants and animals. Many of the plants and animals are **aquatic**, which means they live in water. Some animals, such as this sea lion, can live both in and out of water.

Many kinds of plants and animals can be found along rocky seashores. Some live in water, and others live on shore. All kinds of birds find food along seashores, as well.

TIDES AND TIDE POOLS

Seashores have **tides**. Tides are the rising and falling of the water levels along a seashore. Each seashore has **high tides** and **low tides**. The tides change four times a day. Plants and animals that live along rocky seashores must get used to these changes to stay alive.

A seashore has two high tides and two low tides every day. This picture shows a seashore at high tide. Most of the shore is covered by water.

This is a picture of the same seashore at low tide. Much of the shore is no longer covered by water. It is **exposed**, or open, to the air.

Seashore zones

A seashore has four zones—the **splash zone**, the **upper shore**, the **middle shore**, and the **lower shore**. Different plants and animals live in the different zones. Plants and animals in the higher zones are exposed to the air more often than those in the lower zones.

The splash zone is never covered by water. Only a few waves reach it.

The upper shore is covered during high tide only some of the time.

The middle shore is covered at every high tide. It is exposed to the air at every low tide.

The lower shore is almost always covered by water.

Tide pools

When high tide changes to low tide, water moves away from the shore. As the water moves out to sea, some of it gets trapped among the rocks. The trapped water creates small pools called **tide pools**. Animals often get trapped in tide pools. The pools allow the animals to stay under water during low tide until high tide returns.

Tide pools may be small, but they hold a lot of plant and animal life!

This fish is feeding on a sea urchin to get the nutrients and energy it needs.

WHAT IS A FOOD CHAIN?

Plants and animals are living things. To stay alive, they need sunlight, water, and food. Food provides plants and animals with **nutrients**. Nutrients keep living things healthy.

Food also provides **energy**. Energy gives living things the power to do things. It allows plants and animals to grow. Animals also use energy to breathe, to move, and to find food.

Energy from the sun

Plants do not eat food to get energy and nutrients. They make their own food! Plants use energy from the sun to **produce**, or make, food.

Eating for energy

Animals cannot make food. They must eat to get energy and nutrients. Different animals eat different kinds of foods. Some animals feed on plants. Others eat the plant-eating animals. Some eat both plants and animals. This pattern of eating and being eaten is called a **food chain**. All the living things in a food chain are connected. An example of a seashore food chain is shown on the right.

Starting with the sun

All food chains begin with the sun. Plants trap the sun's energy and use it to make food. They use some of the food energy and store the rest.

When an animal such as a limpet eats plants, it gets some of the energy that was stored in the plants. The limpet gets less of the sun's energy than the plants received.

When a plover eats the limpet, it gets some of the energy that was stored in the limpet. The plover gets less of the sun's energy than the limpet received.

LEVELS IN A FOOD CHAIN

Every food chain has three levels. The first level is made up of plants. Animals that eat plants make up the second level. The third level is made up of animals that eat other animals.

Producing food

Plants are **primary producers**. They are the **primary**, or first, living things in a food chain. Sea grasses are the only true plants in oceans. True plants have stems, roots, and leaves. Seaweeds and other ocean "plants" are actually types of **algae**. Algae are not true plants. They use the sun's energy to make their own food, so they are often called "plants." In this book, the word "plants" refers to both sea grasses and algae.

Eating plants

Herbivores are animals that eat plants. They are **primary consumers**, or the first living things in a food chain that must **consume**, or eat, food to get energy.

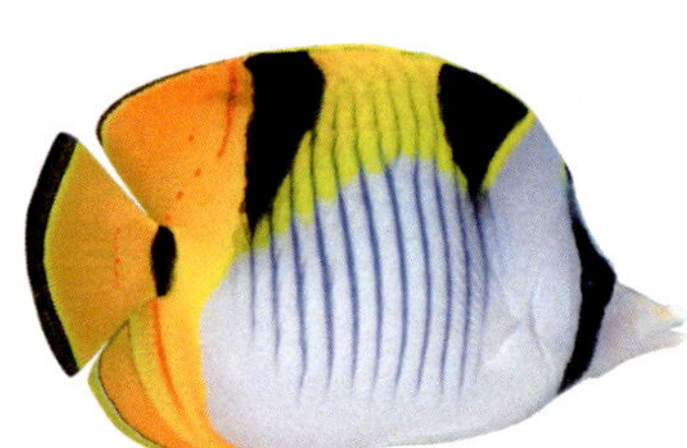

Eating meat

Carnivores, or meat-eaters, make up the third level of a food chain. Carnivores are also called **secondary consumers**. They are the second group of living things in a food chain that must eat food to get energy. Secondary consumers receive only small amounts of the sun's energy from their food.

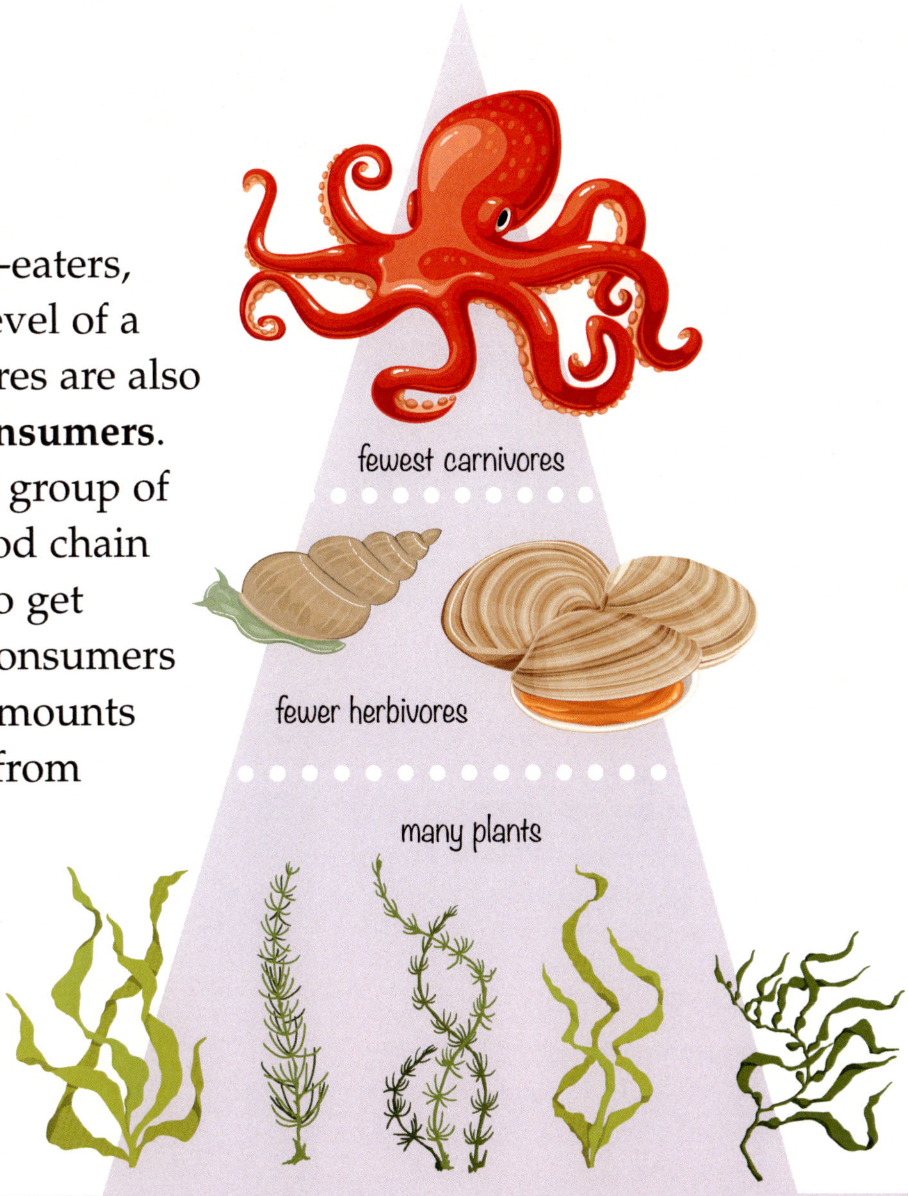

The energy pyramid

An **energy pyramid** shows how energy moves in a food chain. A pyramid is wide at the bottom and narrow at the top. This pyramid is wide at the bottom to show that there are many plants. It takes a lot of plants to make enough energy for the animals in the pyramid. The next level is narrower because there are fewer herbivores than there are plants. There are fewer herbivores because each one must eat many plants to get the energy it needs. The top level of the pyramid is the narrowest because there are fewer carnivores than there are herbivores in a food chain. Each carnivore must eat many herbivores to get the energy it needs.

FOOD FROM THE SUN

Making food using sunlight is called **photosynthesis**. Plants contain **chlorophyll**, which helps photosynthesis take place. Chlorophyll is a green **pigment**, or color, that takes in the sun's energy.

To make food, chlorophyll combines the sun's energy with water, nutrients, and a gas found in air and water. The gas is called **carbon dioxide**. The food that plants make is a type of sugar called **glucose**.

Air to breathe

Large amounts of carbon dioxide are harmful to animals. Aquatic plants take carbon dioxide out of the water during photosynthesis. As they make food, aquatic plants turn carbon dioxide into another gas called oxygen. They release oxygen into the water. Animals must breathe oxygen to survive. Algae make most of the oxygen on Earth that animals and people breathe!

The sun shines on algae and aquatic plants, and they soak up its energy.

Filled with sunlight

People put house plants near windows because plants grow well in warm, sunny spots. Seashores are like the windows of the oceans. The water at seashores is shallow, so sunlight easily reaches the plants that grow on the bottom of an ocean. The sunlight also heats the shallow water, so this water is warmer than the water in the deeper parts of the ocean.

Not just green!

Chlorophyll makes most plants green, but not all algae are green. There are hundreds of different kinds of brown and red algae. These algae contain chlorophyll, but they also have other pigments that make them brown or red.

Kelp, shown right, is a kind of algae. Kelp contains a brown pigment that helps photosynthesis take place in deep water, where there is little sunlight.

PLANTS AND ALGAE

Sea grasses grow along seashores around the world. There are many **species**, or kinds, of sea grasses, but there are thousands of species of algae. Some algae are so tiny that they can be seen only under a microscope!

Some algae are large. Large algae are called seaweeds, but they are not really weeds. These giant algae are also called kelp.

Tiny producers

Phytoplankton are the smallest algae. There can be thousands of phytoplankton in a single drop of water! They float on the ocean's surface, where there is plenty of sunlight for photosynthesis. Billions of phytoplankton live at the surface of an ocean. Most food chains in an ocean start with phytoplankton.

All about algae

Algae are not true plants, but they are like plants. Both plants and algae use photosynthesis to make food, and both are eaten by herbivores. True plants, however, have roots to hold them in place and to absorb nutrients. Algae do not have roots. Many types of algae are **anchored**, or held in one spot, by **holdfasts**. Holdfasts cannot absorb nutrients the way roots can. True plants also have leaves. Seaweeds have leaflike parts called **fronds**. Like leaves, fronds take in sunlight for photosynthesis.

kelp

Some kinds of algae do not have holdfasts. They simply float near the surface of the water.

Kelp is a giant of the algae world. It can grow to be 30 feet (9 m) long!

Bladder wrack and other seaweeds have **air bladders** in their fronds. Having air bladders helps the fronds float, so they are closer to the sunlight.

SEASHORE HERBIVORES

Many kinds of herbivores are found at seashores. The smallest herbivores are **zooplankton**. Zooplankton are tiny animals that can be seen only with a microscope. Zooplankton eat phytoplankton.

Larger herbivores include green sea turtles, sea snails, small fish, and sea urchins. These herbivores eat phytoplankton, as well as larger types of algae.

Green sea turtles are herbivores. They feed on sea grasses that grow in shallow waters at seashores.

Stay away!

Seashore herbivores have many ways to protect themselves from other animals. Some herbivores hide from their enemies. Others have bright colors to warn carnivores that they taste bad or contain poison. Many herbivores have hard shells or cases around their bodies that make it difficult for other animals to eat them.

A sea urchin has spines that protect it from most carnivores. It is not easy for carnivores to eat animals with sharp spines!

Nudibranchs are sea slugs. Their bright colors warn carnivores that these animals have poison in their bodies. Very few carnivores eat nudibranchs.

CARNIVORES AT THE SHORE

Rocky seashores are home to many **predators**. A predator is an animal that hunts and eats other animals, which are called **prey**. Predators are secondary consumers when they hunt and eat herbivores. Secondary consumers include certain fish, lobsters, and octopuses.

When predators hunt and eat other carnivores, they are called **tertiary consumers**. "Tertiary" means "third." Tertiary consumers are the third group of animals in a food chain that must eat to get energy. Some birds and large fish are tertiary consumers.

A giant octopus is a tertiary consumer when it eats another carnivore. This giant octopus is eating a young shark, which is also a carnivore.

Under control

Predators are very important in seashore food chains. They help keep the **populations** of prey animals from growing too large. If too many herbivores lived along a seashore, they would eat all the algae and plants in that area. Sea lions, for example, eat fish, squids, and octopuses. Sea lions help keep the populations of herbivores from growing too large.

The strongest survive

Predators also help keep food chains healthy. They often hunt young, sick, or injured animals. Predators hunt these weak animals because weak animals are the easiest to catch and kill. When weak animals are removed from a food chain, strong, healthy animals have more food to eat.

Sea lions make seashore food chains healthier by eating sick and injured animals.

MANY WAYS TO HUNT

This small snail feeds on barnacles and mussels. Its rough tongue can drill through their shells.

Seashore predators hunt in different ways. Some sneak up on their prey. Others hide and then surprise their prey. Some kill their prey using strength or poison. Many predators simply hunt animals that cannot swim away!

Strong arms

The strong arms of a sea star are covered with hundreds of tiny feet that are like suction cups. The sea star uses its feet to grasp and pull open the shells of scallops. A scallop is very strong, so the starfish can open the shell only a little bit. The sea star then turns its stomach inside out and pushes it into the small opening. It eats the scallop from right inside its shell!

That stings!

A sea anemone is attached to one spot, so it cannot chase its prey. It waits for prey to come to it! An anemone has **tentacles** that sting the shrimps and fish that swim too close. The tentacles stun the prey. The anemone then pulls the prey into its mouth.

What a beak!

Many seabirds have beaks that are shaped to catch and eat their favorite prey. This bird's long, thin beak is perfect for opening an animal's shell.

Well hidden

A flounder has a flat body, and both of its eyes are on one side of its head. This fish lies on the bottom of the ocean and waits for prey to swim by. It then strikes out and surprises its prey with a quick, deadly bite. The flounder is so well hidden in the sand, that predators often do not see it!

EATING EVERYTHING

Many seashore animals are **omnivores**, or animals that eat both plants and animals. Most seashore omnivores are **filter feeders**. Filter feeders suck in water and strain phytoplankton, zooplankton, and other small bits of food from it. Omnivores are also **opportunistic feeders**. Opportunistic feeders are animals that eat any foods that are available.

Raccoons are omnivores that sometimes travel to seashores to eat foods such as sea turtle eggs, crabs, and crayfish.

Most blennies are omnivores. They eat algae and small herbivores.

Sifting for dinner

Some filter feeders, such as barnacles, sea squirts, sponges, and fan worms, cannot move. They are attached to the sea floor or to rocks. To feed, they poke out their legs or tentacles and grab food as it floats past. Other filter feeders eat in a different way. Clams, oysters, and mussels suck in water, strain out the food, and then push out the water.

Sea fans stick out their feathery tentacles to filter food. They pull the tentacles inside their hard tubes when predators are nearby.

Barnacles have legs covered with tiny hairs called *cirri*. A barnacle sweeps its legs through the water, and the cirri trap food.

Sea cucumbers have rings of tentacles around their mouths. They use the tentacles to filter food from the water or to sift bits of food from the sea floor.

CLEAN-UP CREWS

Many animals clean up leftover seashore meals. **Scavengers** are meat-eaters that do not hunt. They eat meat that predators have left behind. Scavengers also feed on the dead animals they find. Certain kinds of crabs, shrimps, and snails are scavengers. Birds such as gulls are also scavengers.

Tiny bits of algae, plants, and animal parts often float away as animals feed in the water. This dead material is called **detritus**. Although it is dead, detritus still contains nutrients and energy. Many filter feeders eat detritus, as well as zooplankton and phytoplankton.

gull

Master recyclers

Hermit crabs are excellent scavengers. They even find ways to use things they cannot eat! These crabs have soft bodies, but they do not have shells. They find the shells of dead snails and wear them as "armor." When the crabs outgrow their borrowed shells, they leave them behind. They then look for larger shells to wear.

Breaking it down

Decomposers are living things that break down any detritus that filter feeders and scavengers do not eat. Most ocean decomposers are tiny living things called **bacteria**. Bacteria can be seen only through a microscope.

Completing the cycle

Decomposers are important. Without them, a lot of energy and nutrients would be wasted. When decomposers break down dead material, leftover nutrients are released into the water. Ocean plants use these nutrients to make the food they need to stay alive. If plants could not make food, they and the many animals that eat plants, would soon die.

A detritus food chain

When living things, such as this eel, die, they become dead material. Scavengers eat the dead material, but bits of detritus are left over.

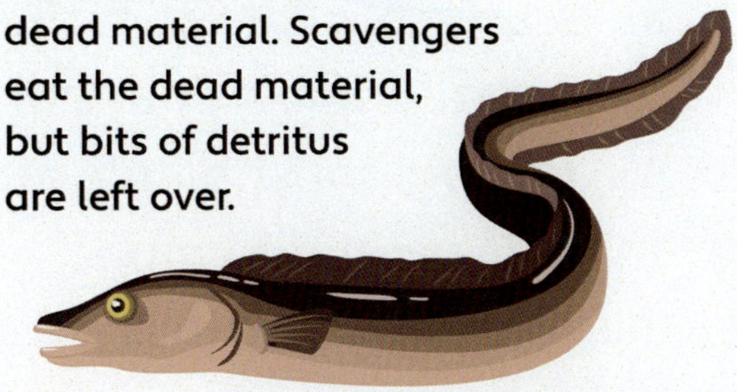

When decomposers such as these bacteria feed on the detritus, they get some of the energy that was trapped in the detritus. Their bodies release part of the nutrients back into the water.

Ocean plants take nutrients from the water. They use the nutrients to grow and to make food.

Note: The arrows point toward the living things that receive energy.

SEASHORE FOOD WEBS

Most animals eat more than one kind of plant or animal. As a result, most plants and animals belong to more than one food chain. When a plant or an animal is part of two or more food chains, those chains are linked together. Linked food chains form a **food web**. All the living things in a food web are connected to one another. If something such as **pollution** affects one part of the web, it will affect the other parts, too.

Lobsters are links in many seashore food chains. They eat sea snails, phytoplankton, zooplankton, shrimps, and algae. Lobsters are eaten by fish, birds, sea otters, and people.

A seashore food web

This diagram shows how living things form a seashore food web when they eat more than one kind of food. The arrows show how energy moves from one living thing to another in the web.

DANGERS TO SEASHORES

Seashores all over the world are at risk because of pollution. Pollution travels easily through water, so it can spread across oceans from one part of the world to another. One type of pollution is caused by **oil spills**.

Oil spills happen when the ships or pipelines that carry oil leak the oil into oceans. The oil washes up along seashores and poisons birds, snails, **shellfish**, and other animals. Near shore, oil can also kill fish.

Black death

After an oil spill, it takes years for the plants and animals in an area to become healthy again. Oil also destroys the waterproof coverings on the fur or feathers of aquatic animals. Without their coverings, these animals cannot stay warm in water, and they die. The cormorant shown below died after being covered with oil from an oil spill.

Polluted water

Pollution is worse near seashores than it is in deep ocean water. Poisonous chemicals from factories often leak into rivers, which carry them to seashores. When an animal eats a poisoned plant or animal, it also gets poisoned. In this way, chemicals spread through many seashore food chains.

Too much algae!

Pesticides and **fertilizers** also end up at seashores. They cause **algae blooms**. Algae blooms are patches of algae that grow out of control. When algae blooms die, they pull most of the oxygen from the surrounding ocean water. Without oxygen, the animals that live in the water cannot breathe. The huge patch of algae shown on the right is too much for the seashore herbivores to eat. When the algae dies, many animals die, too.

SAVING SEASHORES

Many people are working hard to save seashores. Governments protect areas of seashore by making them **national parks**. National parks are closely guarded against pollution, **overfishing**, and other threats.

Environmental groups work to protect seashores, too. They convince governments to pass stricter laws against polluting and overfishing. These groups also educate people about dangers to seashores.

Look, learn, and leave

One important way to help seashores is to learn more about them and then spread the word. You can read books, visit Internet sites, and watch videos about seashores. The best way to learn more about seashores is to visit one. To help protect the seashore, follow these rules during your visit:

- Look at animals without touching them. Just watch the animals to see how they behave and what they do when the tides change.
- Watch where you step–something that looks like a rock could be an animal!
- Take any garbage with you when you leave.

GLOSSARY

Note: Boldfaced words that are defined in the text may not appear in the glossary.

decomposers Living things that eat detritus

detritus Dead material that is breaking down

fertilizer Substances added to soil to help plants grow

holdfasts Parts of algae plants that fasten the algae to rocks or to the sea floor

nutrients Substances in food that help living things grow and stay healthy

overfishing Taking too many of one type of animal from an area of the ocean

pesticide A chemical made to kill insects

pigment A natural color found in plants or animals

pollution Garbage and chemicals that people dump onto land and into water

population The total number of one type of animal living in a certain area

primary producers The first living things in a food chain that can make their own food

shellfish Aquatic animals that live in shells

temperate Describes places that have hot summers and cold winters

tentacle A long, flexible body part used by an animal to grab food

INDEX